The WORL

DAD
JOKES

501 *of the* MOST
GROAN-WORTHY JOKES,
RIDDLES, *and* PUNS EVER TOLD

Edited by Emily McKeon

This Book Belongs to:

_____

_____

Thanks!

Thank you for your purchase. If you enjoyed this book, please consider dropping us a review by scanning the QR code. It takes only 5 seconds and helps small independent publishers like ours.

Scripto Love
PRESS

THE WORLD'S WORST DAD JOKES

Spot illustrations: Creative Fabrica & Freepik.com

CONTENTS

INTRODUCTION

Sit back and enjoy *The World's Best Dad Jokes.* This book is packed with hours of knee-slapping laughter, featuring over 500 jokes, riddles, and puns only a dad could love. Jokes get cornier as each chapter progresses, so they're broken out into three sections: "Bad!", "Terrible!", and "The Worst!" With this many jokes, dad will surely have enough material to elicit groans and eye rolls for years to come!

DAD JOKES & PUNS

BAD!

I'm afraid for the calendar.
Its days are numbered.

Dear Math, grow up and solve
your own problems.

I asked my dog what's two minus two.
He said nothing.

I don't trust stairs.
They're always up to something.

I have a joke about chemistry,
but I don't think it will get a reaction.

I used to be addicted to soap,
but I'm clean now.

Singing in the shower is fun until
you get soap in your mouth.
Then it's a soap opera.

I thought the dryer was shrinking my clothes.
Turns out it was the refrigerator all along.

Shout out to my fingers.
I can count on all of them.

I used to hate facial hair...**but then
it grew on me.**

I decided to sell my vacuum cleaner—
it was just gathering dust!

You think swimming with
sharks is expensive?
You're right. It cost me an arm and a leg.

When two vegans get in an argument,
is it still called a beef?

Do you wanna box for your leftovers?
No, but I'll wrestle you for them.

Dad, did you get a haircut?
"No, I got them all cut!"

Did you hear the rumor about butter?
Well, I'm not going to spread it!

Dad, can you put my shoes on?
"No, I don't think they'll fit me."

If a child refuses to nap,
are they guilty of resisting a rest?

I once got fired from a canned juice company.
Apparently I couldn't concentrate.

I used to play piano by ear.
Now I use my hands.

Have you ever tried to catch a fog?
I tried yesterday but I mist.

I'm on a seafood diet.
I see food and I eat it.

I'm reading a book about anti-gravity.
It's impossible to put down!

I've got a great joke about construction,
but I'm still working on it.

I used to be a personal trainer.
Then I gave my too weak notice.

I'm so good at sleeping,
I can do it with my eyes closed.

Today, my son asked, "Can I have a
bookmark?" I burst into tears—**11 years old
and he still doesn't know my name is Brian.**

The past, the present, and the future
walked into a bar. **It was tense.**

I'm an expert at picking leaves
and heating them in water.
It's my special tea.

**You can't plant flowers
if you haven't botany.**

Police arrested a bottle of water because
it was wanted in three different states:
solid, liquid, and gas.

My son's fourth birthday was today.
When he came to see me, I didn't
recognize him at first.
I had never seen him be four.

A bartender broke up
with her boyfriend,
**but he kept asking her
for another shot.**

My doctor told me I've really grown
as a person. Well, her exact words were
that I **"gained excess weight."**

Did you hear about the
restaurant on the moon?
Great food, no atmosphere.

My kid wants to invent a pencil
with an eraser on each end,
but I just don't see the point.

I spent a lot of time, money, and
effort childproofing my house,
but the kids still get in.

Did you hear about the guy who stole
50 cartons of hand sanitizer?
**They couldn't prosecute—his
hands were clean.**

Did you hear about the aquatic sea
mammals that escaped from the zoo?
It was otter chaos.

My IQ test results came back.
They were negative.

My wife asked me to sync her phone,
so I threw it into the ocean.

My wife is really mad that I have no sense of
direction. **I packed up my stuff and right.**

You know, people say they pick their nose,
but I feel like I was just born with mine.

♛

Can February March?
No, but April May.

Τ

I was just reminiscing about the beautiful
herb garden I had when I was growing up.
Good thymes.

👨

Inflation is really getting out of hand,
but that's just my five cents.

☕

My dentist offered me dentures for only
a dollar. It sounded like a good deal at
the time, **but now I have buck teeth.**

It hurts me to say this,
but I have a sore throat.

I had a date last night. It was perfect.
Tomorrow, I'll try a grape.

I've been breeding racing deer.
Just trying to make a quick buck.

Did you hear about the kidnapping at school?
It's okay, he woke up.

Mountains aren't just funny.
They're hill areas.

Whenever I try to eat healthy,
a chocolate bar looks at me and Snickers.

Spring is here!
I got so excited I wet my plants.

I could tell a joke about pizza,
but it's a little cheesy.

Don't trust atoms.
They make up everything!

Is this pool safe for diving?
It deep ends.

Imagine if you walked into a bar
and there was a long line of people
waiting to take a swing at you.
That's the punch line.

Air used to be free at the gas station,
now it's $1.50. You know why?
Inflation.

I ordered a chicken and an egg from Amazon.
I'll let you know.

I can't take my dog to the pond anymore
because the ducks keep attacking him.
**That's what I get for buying
a pure bread dog.**

My wife said I was immature.
So I told her to get out of my fort.

I didn't want to believe that my dad was
stealing from his job as a traffic cop,
but when I got home, all the signs were there.

A cheese factory exploded in France.
Da Brie is everywhere!

I was really angry at my friend Mark
for stealing my dictionary.
I told him, "Mark, my words!"

Not sure if you have noticed, but I love
bad puns. **That's just how eye roll.**

TERRIBLE!

I like telling Dad jokes.
Sometimes he laughs!

I slept like a log last night.
Woke up in the fireplace!

If towels could tell jokes, **I think they'd
have a very dry sense of humor.**

The wedding was so beautiful,
even the cake was in tiers.

I used to run a dating service for chickens.
But I was struggling to make hens meet.

Within minutes, the detectives knew
what the murder weapon was.
It was a brief case.

Not to brag but I made six figures last year.
**I was also named worst employee
at the toy factory.**

To whoever stole my copy of
Microsoft Office, I will find you.
You have my Word!

I used to work in a shoe-recycling shop.
It was sole destroying.

My boss told me to have a good day,
so I went home.

I thought about going on an
all-almond diet... **But that's just nuts.**

My friend asked me, "What rhymes with orange?"
And I told him, "No, it doesn't!"

My wife told me I had to stop acting like
a flamingo. **So I put my foot down.**

I told my wife she drew her
eyebrows too high.
She seemed surprised.

I tell dad jokes but I have no kids...
I'm a faux pa.

If you see a robbery at an Apple Store
does that make you an iWitness?

Five out of four people admit they're
bad with fractions.

I'll call you later.
Don't call me later, call me Dad!

Did you hear about the
Italian chef who died?
He pasta way.

I don't play soccer because I enjoy the sport.
I'm just doing it for kicks.

I invented a new word today: **plagiarism!**

After dinner, my wife asked
if I could clear the table.
I needed a running start, but I made it.

I know a lot of jokes about retired people
but none of them work.

I accidentally dropped my pillow on the floor.
I think it has a concushion.

Someone complimented my parking today.
**They left a sweet note on my windshield
that said "parking fine."**

St. Francis worked at Krispy Kreme.
He was a deep friar.

My hotel tried to charge me $10 extra for
air conditioning. **That wasn't cool.**

I hate it when people say age is only a number.
Age is clearly a word.

An apple a day keeps the doctor away.
At least it does if you throw it hard enough.

I asked my date to meet me at the
gym but she never showed up.
**I guess the two of us aren't
going to work out.**

Did you hear about the ATM
that got addicted to money?
It suffered from withdrawals.

If an English teacher is convicted of
a crime and doesn't complete the
sentence, **is that a fragment?**

I think my wife is putting glue on
my antique weapons collection.
**She denies it, but I'm sticking
to my guns!**

I don't really care for funerals
that start before noon.
I guess I'm just not a mourning person.

One of my favorite memories as a kid
was when my brothers used to put me
inside a tire and roll me down a hill.
They were Goodyears.

I never buy pre-shredded cheese.
Doing it yourself is grate.

I was playing chess with my friend and
he said, "Let's make this interesting."
So we stopped playing chess.

I have a great joke about nepotism.
But I'll only tell it to my kids.

Have you heard about those
new corduroy pillows?
They're making headlines.

So a vowel saves another vowel's life.
The other vowel says, **"Aye E! I owe you!"**

Did I tell you the time I fell in love during
a backflip? **I was heels over head.**

When I was a kid, my mother told me
I could be anyone I wanted to be.
Turns out, identity theft is a crime.

I once wrote a song about a tortilla,
but it's more of a wrap.

If the early bird catches the worm,
I'll sleep in until there are pancakes.

Did you know that milk is the
fastest liquid on earth?
**It's pasteurized before you
can even see it.**

Did you hear about the circus fire?
It was in tents.

Wanna hear a joke about paper?
Never mind—it's tearable.

I wouldn't buy anything with velcro.
It's a total rip-off.

Dogs can't operate MRI machines.
But catscan.

Sundays are always a little sad,
but the day before is a sadder day.

Did you hear about the power outlet
who got into a fight with a power cord?
He thought he could socket to him.

I only seem to get sick on weekdays.
I must have a weekend immune system.

My friend was showing me his tool shed and
pointed to a ladder. **"That's my stepladder,"
he said. "I never knew my real ladder."**

I just found out I'm colorblind.
The news came out of the purple!

Did you know your pupils are the last
part to stop working when you die?
They dilate.

My wife asked me the other day
where I got so much candy. I said,
"I always have a few Twix up my sleeve."

I hate my job—all I do is crush cans all day.
It's soda pressing.

Of all the inventions of the last 100 years,
**the dry erase board has to be the
most remarkable.**

Did you know that the first french fries
weren't cooked in France?
They were cooked in Greece.

I found a wooden shoe in my toilet today.
It was clogged.

If prisoners could take their own mug shots
they'd be called cell-fies.

If a pig loses its voice
does it become disgruntled?

I don't get why bakers aren't wealthier.
They make so much dough.

I just applied for a job down at the diner.
I told them I really bring a lot to the table.

I'm Buzz Aldrin, second man
to step on the moon.
Neil before me.

If you're feeling depressed, try drinking
a gallon of water before you go to sleep.
**It'll give you a reason to get out of bed
in the morning.**

My landlord told me we need to
talk about the heating bill.
"Sure," I said. "My door is always open."

I built a model of Mount Everest
and my son asked if it was to scale.
"No," I said. "It's to look at."

My friend claims he glued himself to his
autobiography. I don't believe him,
but that's his story and he's sticking to it.

A century ago, two brothers
decided it was possible to fly.
And as you can see, they were Wright.

I just spent $300 on a limo and learned
it doesn't come with a driver.
**I can't believe I have nothing
to chauffer it.**

I have a joke about trickle down economics.
But 99% of you will never get it.

I have a joke about trickle down economics.

A buddy asked how many fish I caught.
I told him it's not polite to fish and tell.

I tried to start a professional hide
and seek team, but it didn't work out.
Turns out, good players are hard to find.

A cop started crying while he was
writing me a ticket. I asked him why and
he said, **"It's a moving violation."**

Swords will never go obsolete.
They're cutting edge technology.

THE WORST!

I went to a smoke shop only to discover
it'd been replaced by an apparel store.
Clothes, but no cigar.

My wife gave me an ultimatum:
her or my addiction to sweets.
The decision was a piece of cake.

The guy who stole my diary just died.
My thoughts are with his family.

My wife left a note on the fridge
that said, "This isn't working."
I'm not sure what she's talking about.
I opened the fridge door and it's working fine!

My parents raised me as an only child.
Which really annoyed my younger brother.

Did you hear about the chameleon
who couldn't change color?
He had a reptile dysfunction.

I wanted to go on a diet,
but I feel like I have way too much
on my plate right now.

This graveyard looks overcrowded.
People must be dying to get in there.

The shovel was a **groundbreaking invention**.

Does anyone need an ark?
I Noah guy!

I've never gone to a gun range before.
I decided to give it a shot.

A furniture store keeps calling me.
All I wanted was one night stand.

I'm thinking about removing my spine.
I feel like it's only holding me back.

My extra winter weight is finally gone.
Now, I have spring rolls.

I bought the world's worst
thesaurus yesterday.
Not only is it terrible, it's terrible.

I saw a 1,000-year-old oil stain;
it was from ancient Greece.

Whoever stole my depression
medication — **I hope you're happy now.**

I used to shower at night as a kid,
then I started showering in the morning.
The difference was night and day.

I told my wife she needs to start embracing her mistakes.
So she hugged me.

My wife and I let astrology get between us.
It Taurus apart.

People are usually shocked when they find out...**I'm a bad electrician.**

Just paid $200 for a belt that doesn't fit!
What a huge waist!

Lost my job at the bank on my first day. A woman asked me to check her balance, **so I pushed her over.**

Did you hear the joke about the wandering nun?
She was a Roman Catholic.

I went to a seafood disco last week.
Pulled a mussel.

Sore throats are a pain in the neck.

I can kayak. **Canoe?**

I have a fear of elevators,
but I've started taking steps to avoid it.

I have a clean conscience—**it's never
been used**.

How do I look? **With your eyes.**

My wife said I should do lunges
to stay in shape.
That would be a big step forward.

I'm starting my new job at a restaurant
next week. **I can't wait.**

Do I enjoy making courthouse puns?
Guilty.

Someone has glued my pack
of cards together—**I don't know how
to deal with it**.

I have a fear of speed bumps.
I'm slowly getting over it.

I used to be addicted to the hokey pokey,
but then I turned myself around.

Time to take this cookie to the hospital.
It's feeling crummy.

I never thought orthopedic shoes
would work for me.
But I stand corrected.

Did you hear about the guy who
invented Lifesavers?
They say he made a mint.

My dad told me a joke about boxing.
I guess I missed the punchline.

I just got a promotion at the farm.
Now I'm the C-I-E-I-O.

To the person who stole my place
in the queue – **I'm after you now**.

Stop looking for the perfect
match – **use a lighter**.

Did you hear about the guy who
invented the knock-knock joke?
He won the 'no-bell' prize.

My kids think I use outdated technology.
But they're just ignoring the fax.

So what if I don't know what
"Armageddon" means?
It's not the end of the world.

Don't you hate it when someone answers
their own questions? **I do.**

My uncle named his dogs Rolex and Timex.
They're his watch dogs.

Time flies like an arrow,
fruit flies like a banana.

A man is washing his car with his son.
The son asks, **"Can't you just use a sponge?"**

Did you hear about the cold dinner?
It was chili.

Did you hear about the ice
cream truck accident?
It crashed on a rocky road.

Did you hear about the whale that
swallowed a clown?
It felt funny after.

I used to be a banker, **but I lost interest.**

Getting paid to sleep
would be my dream job.

Did you hear the one about
the dog and the tree?
They had a long conversation about bark.

The average person is really mean.

I'd never let my children watch
the orchestra.
There's too much sax and violins.

I just saw my wife trip and fall while carrying
a laundry basket full of ironed clothes.
I watched it all unfold.

My favorite time on the clock is 6:30.
Hands down.

Did you know that if a piano falls on you,
your head will B-flat?

I love my furniture.
My recliner and I go way back.

I haven't been to the gym in so long
I've gone back to calling it James.

Three guys walked into a bar.
You'd think one of them would have seen it.

I just burnt my Hawaiian pizza.
**I guess I should have put it on
aloha temperature.**

I sympathize with batteries.
I'm never included in anything either.

I have submitted 10 jokes now trying to
reach the front page...**no pun in ten did.**

A priest, a pastor, and a rabbit entered a
clinic to donate blood. The nurse asked
the rabbit: "What's your blood type?"
"I'm probably a type O, said the rabbi.

≡ DAD ≡ RIDDLES

BAD!

Why do fathers take an extra pair of socks when they go golfing?

In case they get a hole in one.

What do a tick and the Eiffel Tower have in common?

They're both Paris sites.

If April showers bring May flowers, what do May flowers bring?

Pilgrims.

What do you call a factory that makes okay products?

A satis-factory.

Why do seagulls fly over the ocean?

Because if they flew over the bay,
we'd call them bagels.

How does the moon cut his hair?

Eclipse it.

What did Baby Corn say to Mama Corn?

"Where's Pop Corn?"

Where do you learn to make a banana split?

Sundae school.

What does a lemon say when it answers the phone?

"Yellow!"

How does a taco say grace?

"Lettuce pray."

What time did the man go to the dentist?

Tooth hurt-y.

What concert costs just 45 cents?

50 Cent featuring Nickelback.

What does a bee use to brush its hair?

A honeycomb.

How do you make a tissue dance?

You put a little boogie in it.

What do you call cheese that isn't yours?

Nacho cheese.

How does a penguin build its house?

Igloos it together.

Why did the scarecrow win an award?

Because he was outstanding in his field.

What do you get from a pampered cow?

Spoiled milk.

What's the best smelling insect?

A deodor-ant.

**How many paranoids does it take
to change a light bulb?**

Who wants to know?

What's a vampire's favorite ship?

A blood vessel.

**What happens when it rains cats
and dogs?**

You have to be careful not to
step in a poodle.

What do you call a fish with no eye?

A fsh.

What do you call a lazy kangaroo?

Pouch potato.

Why is grass so dangerous?

Because it's full of blades.

What did one DNA say to the other DNA?

"Do these genes make me look fat?"

Did you hear the joke about experiencing déjà vu?

Did you hear the joke about experiencing déjà vu?

**Why did Beethoven get rid
of his chickens?**

All they said was, "Bach, Bach, Bach..."

I shouldn't have had the sea food.

Now I'm feeling a little eel.

Why do melons have weddings?

Because they cantaloupe.

What do Bostonians call a fake noodle?

An impasta.

Why was the pig covered in ink?

Because it lived in a pen.

What do you call a snitching scientist?

A lab rat.

Why do nurses like red crayons?

Sometimes they have to draw blood.

What do you call a bear with no teeth?

A gummy bear.

If athletes get athlete's foot, what do astronauts get?

Missile toe.

What's a robot's favorite snack?

Computer chips.

What did one cannibal say to the other while they were eating a clown?

"Does this taste funny to you?"

What does garlic do when it gets hot?

It takes its cloves off.

What do you call someone with no body and no nose?

Nobody knows.

Where do math teachers go on vacation?

Times Square.

How can you tell if a tree is a dogwood tree?

By its bark.

**What do you call a hot dog
on wheels?**

Fast food.

Where do young trees go to learn?

Elemen-tree school.

**When does a joke become
a dad joke?**

When it becomes apparent.

What did the coffee report to the police?

A mugging.

Why are elevator jokes so classic?

They work on many levels.

Why is it a bad idea to iron your four-leaf clover?

'Cause you shouldn't press your luck.

What rock group has four men that don't sing?

Mount Rushmore.

Why couldn't the bicycle stand up by itself?

It was two tired.

What happens when you go to the bathroom in France?

European.

How many apples grow on a tree?

All of them!

Why did the invisible man turn down the job offer?

He couldn't see himself doing it!

Why did the old man fall in the well?

Because he couldn't see that well.

Why couldn't the astronaut land on the moon?

Because it was full.

Why do dogs float in water?

Because they are good buoys.

**What kind of music did the
pilgrims listen to?**

Plymouth rock.

**What do you call a shoe made
of a banana?**

A slipper.

**What is the tallest building
in the world?**

The library—it's got the most stories.

**What do you call a beehive
without an exit?**

Unbelievable.

Why was the coach yelling at a vending machine?

He wanted his quarter back.

What do you call a fish wearing a bowtie?

Sofishticated.

Why couldn't the green pepper practice archery?

Because it didn't habanero.

Why did the stadium get so hot after the game?

Because all the fans left.

Why do trees seem suspicious on sunny days?

They just seem a little shady.

After an unsuccessful harvest, why did the farmer decide to try a career in music?

Because he had a ton of sick beets.

How many tickles does it take to make an octopus laugh?

Ten tickles.

What do you call a guy with a rubber toe?

Roberto.

Which days are the strongest?

Saturday and Sunday. The rest are weak days.

Which U.S. state is famous for its extra-small soft drinks?

Minnesota.

What did the ranch say when someone opened the refrigerator door?

"Close the door, I'm dressing!"

What do you call a sad cup of coffee?

Depresso.

What did the policeman say to his belly button?

"You're under a vest!"

TERRIBLE!

**What do scholars eat when
they're hungry?**

Academia nuts.

∞

**What's the difference between a
poorly dressed man on a tricycle and
a well-dressed man on a bicycle?**

Attire.

♔

**What do you call a mac 'n' cheese
that gets all up in your face?**

Too close for comfort food.

**What do sprinters eat
before a race?**

Nothing, they fast.

How do celebrities stay so cool?

They have many fans.

**What did the fisherman say
to the magician?**

"Pick a cod, any cod."

How do you organize a space party?

You planet.

**What does a baby computer
call his father?**

Data.

Why can't a leopard hide?

Because he's always spotted.

How do moths swim?

Using the butterfly stroke.

What do you call an illegally parked frog?

Toad.

How do lawyers say goodbye?

"We'll be suing ya!"

Which bear is the most condescending?

A pan-duh.

**What kind of drink can be
bitter and sweet?**

Reali-tea.

Where do fruits go on vacation?

Pear-is.

What kind of cars do eggs drive?

Yolkswagens.

Which is faster, hot or cold?

Hot, because you can catch a cold.

Where do baby cats learn to swim?

The kitty pool.

Why is cold water so insecure?

Because it's never called hot.

What did the nose tell the finger?

"Stop picking on me."

What do you call a line of men waiting to get haircuts?

A barber-queue.

How can a leopard change his spots?

By moving.

What's an astronaut's favorite part of a computer?

The space bar.

What do you call a Frenchman wearing sandals?

Philippe Flop.

Why is it so cheap to throw a party at a haunted house?

Because the ghosts bring all the boos.

How do cows stay up to date?

They read the moo-spaper.

Where do pirates get their hooks?

Second hand stores.

Why are skeletons so calm?

Because nothing gets under their skin.

Who were the greenest Presidents in US history?

The Bushes.

What is a guitar player's favorite Italian food?

Strum-boli.

What's a lawyer's favorite drink?

Subpoena colada.

What's blue and not very heavy?

Light blue.

How do you make a water bed bouncier?

Add spring water.

What did one monocle say to the other monocle?

Let's get together and make a spectacle of ourselves.

What's the best thing about living in Switzerland?

I don't know, but the flag is a big plus.

Where do dads store their dad jokes?

In the dad-a-base.

What kind of fruit do ghosts like?

Boo-berries.

**What do you call it when
James Bond takes a bath?**

Bubble 07.

Why is it a bad idea to eat a clock?

Because it's so time-consuming.

**What do you call someone who
refuses to fart in public?**

A private tutor.

What do you call bears with no ears?

B.

What does a nosy pepper do?

It gets jalapeno business.

Why didn't the astronaut come home to his wife?

He needed his space.

"Dad, can you explain to me what a solar eclipse is?"

"No sun."

What did the buffalo say to his son when he dropped him off at school?

"Bison."

What did the drummer call his twin daughters?

Anna one, Anna two!

**What's that Nevada city where
all the dentists visit?**

Floss Vegas.

Why did the picture go to jail?

Because it was framed.

How do you make holy water?

You boil the hell out of it.

What do you call a fish with two knees?

A two-knee fish.

**What's black and white and goes
around and around?**

A penguin in a revolving door.

Why don't skeletons ever go trick-or-treating?

Because they have no body to go with.

What do you call an elephant that doesn't matter?

An irrelephant.

What do you call a baby monkey?

A chimp off the old block.

Why are cats bad storytellers?

Because they only have one tale.

Why was the belt sent to jail?

For holding up a pair of pants.

What lies at the bottom of the ocean and twitches?

A nervous wreck.

What kind of dogs do magicians like?

Labracadabradors.

What did the duck say after he finished dinner?

"Put it on my bill."

What awards do dentists receive?

Plaques.

Why are volcanoes so popular?

They are lava-able.

**Why are circles bad at
telling stories?**

Because they are pointless.

**Why did the computer go
to the doctor?**

It had a virus.

**How do you keep a bagel from
running away?**

Put lox on it.

**Which season do people get
injured the most?**

The fall.

Where do pencils come from?

Pennsylvania.

Which state has the most streets?

Rhode Island.

Why are oranges so slow?

They always run out of juice.

How do billboards talk to each other?

Sign language.

What falls in winter but never gets hurt?

Snow.

How do you stop a bull from charging?

Take away its credit cards.

∞

What's the best kind of music to listen to when fishing?

Something catchy.

What's the best kind of bird to work for a construction company?

A crane.

What did the T-Rex use to cut wood?

A dino-saw.

**Why did the man put his money
in the freezer?**

He wanted cold, hard cash.

**What kind of music do
chiropractors like?**

Hip pop.

When does it rain money?

When there is a change in the weather.

**How did the pirate get his ship
for so cheap?**

It was on sail.

Why are plants so thin?

They are light eaters.

Where do boats go when they're sick?

To the dock.

How was Rome split in two?

With a pair of Ceasars.

Why are spiders so smart?

They can find everything on the web.

What did the shy pebble wish for?

That he was a little boulder.

What did one hat say to the other?

"Stay here, I'm going on ahead."

THE WORST!

**What do you say to your sister
when she's crying?**

"Are you having a crisis?"

ᴖᴖ

**What do you call Batman
when he's hurt?**

Bruised Wayne.

♔

**Why did the spoon come to the
party dressed as a knife?**

The invitation said to look sharp.

What is the fastest growing city in the world?

Capital of Ireland – it's Dublin everyday.

Why don't they play poker in the jungle?

Too many cheetahs.

When is a door not a door?

When it's ajar.

When do computers overheat?

When they need to vent.

What do you call a mountain of cats?

Meow-tain.

Why don't eggs tell jokes?

They'd crack each other up.

Why do we tell actors to break a leg?

Because every play has a cast.

**What do prisoners use
to call each other?**

Cell phones.

Why were they called the Dark Ages?

Because there were a lot of knights.

What is the opposite of a croissant?

A happy uncle.

Which branch of the military accepts toddlers?

The infantry.

How does a computer get drunk?

It takes screenshots.

Why did Shakespeare's wife leave him?

She got sick of all the drama.

Where do horses live?

In neigh-borhoods.

Why are piggy banks so wise?

They're filled with common cents.

What did one pirate say to the other when he beat him at chess?

"Checkmatey."

Why did the baby strawberry cry?

His parents were in a jam.

What kind of jewelry do rabbits wear?

14 carrot gold.

What do you call an unpredictable camera?

A loose Canon.

How do you fix a cracked pumpkin?

With a pumpkin patch.

How do you get a country girl's attention?

A-tractor.

How do snails fight?

They slug it out.

Why can't you trust duck doctors?

They're all quacks.

What do you call a priest who becomes a lawyer?

A father-in-law.

Why do cows have hooves and not feet?

They lactose.

Why couldn't the couple get married at the library?

It was all booked up.

Why did the restaurant hire a pig?

He was good at bacon.

How does Moses make his coffee?

Hebrews it.

How does a rancher keep track of his cattle?

With a cow-culator.

Why should you never use "beef stew" as a password?

It's not stroganoff.

What do you call an alligator detective?

An investi-gator.

What do horses say when they fall?

"I can't giddy up."

What has four wheels and flies?

A garbage truck.

Why didn't the skeleton get a prom date?

He didn't have the guts to ask anyone.

**What did the yoga instructor say
when her landlord tried to evict her?**

"Namaste."

Why don't crabs give to charity?

Because they're shell-fish.

Why are toilets always so good at poker?

They always get a flush.

What kind of bird is always getting hurt?

The owl.

What did the slow tomato say to the others?

"Don't worry, I'll ketchup."

What do you call a pony with a sore throat?

A little hoarse.

Why do pancakes always win at baseball?

They have the best batter.

What kind of noise does a witch's vehicle make?

Brrrrooom, brrrooom.

Why was Cinderella thrown off the football team?

She ran away from the ball.

How does Darth Vader like his toast?

On the dark side.

Where do sharks go on vacation?

Finland.

**What kind of shoes do
ninjas wear?**

Sneakers.

**What did the grape do when he
got stepped on?**

He let out a little wine.

**Why are pediatricians always
so angry?**

Because they have little patients.

What kind of magazines do cows read?

Cattlelogs.

What do lazy farmers grow?

Couch potatoes.

**What do you call a can opener
that doesn't work?**

A can't opener.

What should you do if you meet a giant?

Use big words.

**What's the best air to breathe if you
want to be rich?**

Millionaire.

What kind of music scares balloons?

Pop music.

What did one wall say to the other?

"I'll meet you at the corner."

Why did the banana go to the doctor?

Because it wasn't peeling well.

Why did the watch go on vacation?

To unwind.

Why did the computer get glasses?

To improve its web-site.

What did the blanket say to the bed?

"I've got you covered."

Why are fish so easy to weigh?

Because they have their own set of scales.

**What do you give a scientist
with bad breath?**

Experi-mints.

How much money does a skunk have?

Just one scent.

How do you get a mouse to smile?

Say "cheese."

What did one leaf say to the other?

"I'm falling for you."

Why do hamburgers go south for the winter?

So they don't freeze their buns.

Why did the whale blush?

It saw the ocean's bottom.

Why couldn't the toilet paper cross the road?

It got stuck in a crack.

Why didn't the sun go to college?

It already had a million degrees.

What do you call someone who can't stick to a diet?

A desserter.

Where's the one place you should never take your dog?

A flea market.

Where do elephants store luggage?

In a trunk.

What did the Dalmatian say after dinner?

"That hit the spot."

**What does a painter do
when he gets cold?**

Put on another coat.

**Where do books hide when
they're afraid?**

Under their covers.

What time do ducks wake up?

At the quack of dawn.

What kind of tree fits in your hand?

A palm tree.

What do you call a fibbing cat?

A lion.

Why was the broom late?

It over-swept.

☉☉

When at night do parents change the most diapers?

In the wee wee hours.

☉☉

How do flat-earthers travel?

On a plane.

☉☉

Why wasn't one Father's Day gift any better than the other?

It was a tie.

≡ DAD ≡ KNOCK KNOCK JOKES

BAD!

Knock, knock!

Who's there?

Kenya.

Kenya who?

Kenya stop with the jokes already?

Knock, knock!

Who's there?

Jewel.

Jewel who?

Jewel be happy to know it's Friday!

Knock, knock!

Who's there?

Arthur.

Arthur who?

Arthur any more knock-knock jokes?

Knock, knock!

Who's there?

Beak.

Beak who?

Beak careful, that pan is hot!

Knock, knock!

Who's there?

Tuna.

Tuna who?

Tuna piano if it sounds off-key.

Knock, knock!

Who's there?

Fur.

Fur who?

Fur you, anything!

Knock, knock!

Who's there?

Knew.

Knew who?

Knew you'd have to ask.

Knock, knock!

Who's there?

S'more.

S'more who?

S'more jokes on the way.

Knock, knock!

Who's there?

Ivanna.

Ivanna who?

Ivanna hold your hand.

❧

Knock, knock!

Who's there?

Spell.

Spell who?

Sure, W-H-O.

❧

Knock, knock!

Who's there?

Cash.

Cash who?

No thanks, I like almonds.

Knock, knock!

Who's there?

Yeah.

Yeah who?

Yahoo, I'm excited too!

Knock, knock!

Who's there?

Annie.

Annie who?

Annie one you want me to be.

Knock, knock!

Who's there?

Candice.

Candice who?

Candice be over already?

Knock, knock!

Who's there?

Luke.

Luke who?

Luke for yourself, I'm busy.

❦

Knock, knock!

Who's there?

Daryl.

Daryl who?

Daryl never be anyone like you.

❦

Knock, knock!

Who's there?

Launch.

Launch who?

Launch is my favorite meal.

TERRIBLE!

Knock, knock!

Who's there?

May fourth.

May fourth who?

May the fourth be with you.

Knock, knock!

Who's there?

Bear.

Bear who?

Bear with me, we aren't done yet.

Knock, knock!

Who's there?

Ash.

Ash who?

Gesundheit! Need a tissue?

👨

Knock, knock!

Who's there?

Tank.

Tank who?

You're welcome.

👨

Knock, knock!

Who's there?

Mustache.

Mustache who?

I mustache you a question!

Knock, knock!

Who's there?

Ben.

Ben who?

**Ben out here knocking
forever, let me in!**

♦♦

Knock, knock!

Who's there?

Wayne.

Wayne who?

Wayne drops keep falling on my head.

♦♦

Knock, knock.

Who's there?

Butter.

Butter who?

Butter hurry and let them in!

Knock, knock!

Who's there?

Aida.

Aida who?

Aida big dinner and now I'm full.

Knock, knock!

Who's there?

Lettuce.

Lettuce who?

Lettuce in, it's cold out here!

Knock, knock!

Who's there?

Says.

Says who?

Says me!

Knock, knock!

Who's there?

Olive.

Olive who?

Olive knock-knock jokes!

Knock, knock!

Who's there?

Harmony.

Harmony who?

Harmony knock-knock jokes can one person tell?

Knock, knock!

Who's there?

Frank.

Frank who?

Frank you for asking, it's me.

Knock, knock!

Who's there?

Francis.

Francis who?

Franc-is my favorite country.

Knock, knock!

Who's there?

Opportunity.

Opportunity who?

When opportunity knocks, you answer.

Knock, knock!

Who's there?

Teddy.

Teddy who?

Teddy's my birthday. Woohoo!

THE WORST!

Knock, knock!

Who's there?

Honey.

Honey who?

Honey, I'm home.

👨

Knock, knock!

Who's there?

Len.

Len who?

Len me some money, please.

Knock, knock!

Who's there?

Ketchup.

Ketchup who?

Ketchup with you later.

☙

Knock, knock!

Who's there?

A little old lady.

A little old lady who?

I didn't know you could yodel!

☙

Knock, knock!

Who's there?

Lena.

Lena who?

**Lena bit closer,
I have something to tell you.**

Knock, knock!

Who's there?

Abby.

Abby who?

Abby just stung me, ouch!

Knock, knock!

Who's there?

Giraffe.

Giraffe who?

Giraffe anything else to say?

Knock, knock!

Who's there?

Some bunny.

Some bunny who?

Some bunny who loves you.

Knock, knock!

Who's there?

Iran.

Iran who?

Iran all the way home.

Knock, knock!

Who's there?

Sia.

Sia who?

Sia later!

Knock, knock!

Who's there?

Yetta.

Yetta who?

Yetta another knock-knock joke.

Printed in Great Britain
by Amazon